bush
PUBLISHING
& associates

FAITH that PLEASES

Sheila Green

Unless otherwise noted, all Scripture quotations are from the King James Version of the Bible.

All Scripture quotations marked AMP are taken from The Amplified Bible, New Testament. Copyright © 1958, 1987 by The Lockman Foundation, La Habra, California.

Scripture quotations marked The Message are taken from THE MESSAGE. Copyright © 1993, 1994, 1995, 1996, 2000, 2001, 2002 by Eugene H. Peterson. Used by permission of NavPress Publishing Group.

All Scripture quotations marked NKJV are taken from the New King James Version of the Bible. Copyright © 1979, 1980, 1982, Thomas Nelson, Inc., Publishers.

All Scripture quotations marked NLT are taken from the Holy Bible, New Living Translation, copyright © 1996. Used by permission of Tyndale House Publishers, Inc., Wheaton, Illinois 60189. All rights reserved.

All Scripture quotations marked ESV are taken from The Holy Bible, English Standard Version. Copyright © 2001 by Crossway Bibles, a division of Good News Publishers.

All Scripture quotations marked NIV are taken from The Holy Bible: New International Version® NIV®. Copyright © 1973, 1978, 1984 by International Bible Society. Used by permission of Zondervan Publishing House. All rights reserved.

All Scripture quotations marked RSV are taken from The Revised Standard Version of the Bible. Copyright © 1946, Old Testament Section. Copyright © 1952 by the Division of Christian Education of the Churches of Christ in the United States of America.

All Scripture quotations marked NASB are taken from The New American Standard Bible. Copyright © 1960, 1962, 1963, 1968, 1971, 1972, 1973, 1975, 1977, by the Lockman Foundation. La Habra, California.

The Living Bible copyright © 1971 by Tyndale House Foundation. Used by permission of Tyndale House Publishers Inc., Carol Stream, Illinois 60188. All rights reserved. The Living Bible, TLB, and the The Living Bible logo are registered trademarks of Tyndale House Publishers.

Faith That Pleases
Copyright © 2015 Sheila Green
ISBN: 978-0-9967285-0-8

Bush Publishing & Associates books may be ordered at www.BushPublishing.com or www.Amazon.com. For further information, please contact:

Bush Publishing & Associates
www.BushPublishing.com

Because of the dynamic nature of the Internet, any web address or link contained in this book may have changed since publication and may no longer be valid.

Printed in the United States of America. No portion of this book may be used or reproduced by any means: graphic, electronic or mechanical, including photocopying, recording, taping, or by any information storage retrieval system, without the written permission of the publisher, except in the case of brief quotations embodied in critical articles and reviews.

DEDICATION

First and foremost, I can do nothing apart from God. He is the reason this book is here. He is My God that I lean on, trust and can't live without. This book is His idea. To God be the Glory!

Second, life's struggles, they taught me how to go after God to survive.

Third, Family Life Church that provided life groups to be a part of, to grow and seek God. A special thank you to Thomas and Cindy Bihm for leading and ministering in the Submerge life group, God has truly used your ministry for His glory!

To my precious husband and daughter, Kevin & Rebekah, I love you both so much, thank you for loving me.

CONTENTS

INTRODUCTION	1
DEVOTIONS	3
Would You Like to Be Wise?	5
Put the Pen to the Paper	6
All I Am Is in You	7
Prayer of Honor	8
The Earthly Things	9
By Faith	10
Jesus Is my All	11
Dressed With no Place to Go	12
Jesus Lives	13
Yes, It Is Mine	15
My Father Is the Lord!	16
Jesus Is Lord	17
Reigning King	18
Sweet Surrender	19
The Battle	20
Your "Who" Is Not Your "Do!	22
The Well Is Deep	24
Jesus Is the Lover of My Soul	26

Rest in Knowing	27
Inspiration Has to Come	28
My Grace Is Sufficient for You	30
Lord, I Am Renewed	32
What Can I Do to Please God?	34
My Trust Is in the Lord	36
Rest in the Knowing	38
I Am Worthy Because of Jesus	39
Rest in Knowing	41
The Wait Is Real	42
When You Can Do Nothing	43
Today Is a New Day	44
My Life Is not My Own	45
Rest in Knowing	47
My Dependence Is on the Lord	48
I Have Nothing Until I OBEY	49
Nothing	50
Today Is a New Day	52
Waiting Is Important	54
Sit at My Feet and Learn from Me	55
Frustration	57
Destiny	59
Your Dependency Is on Me	61
Your Obedience Is Overwhelming	62
ABOUT THE AUTHOR	66

INTRODUCTION

Living in today's world, for most people, is a struggle. We are always pulled from here to there, trying to balance life in a way that we can do what God has called us to do. The hardest thing is to fit God into our daily routine. But in reality, if we put Him first on our list of things to do, the rest of our day will work out wonderfully. If we just try to fit him in somewhere, there will be more struggles and we won't be capable of handling them.

When we go to Him first, we learn to allow Him to handle our struggles, by releasing them into His care. How can we know God's plan for our lives, if we don't go to Him? We must spend time with Him, and wait for His leading to know His will for our lives. Faith that pleases God, pursues Him.

DEVOTIONS

Would You Like to Be Wise?

Day 1

The Bible says that to know Christ is the beginning of wisdom. It also says that fools say there is no God, and that is exactly why they are not wise. It is impossible to remain wise if you do not know Christ because the beginning of wisdom is to fear and reverence the Lord. Yes, it is.

How can you know Christ? First, you must believe that Jesus is the Christ, the Anointed one of God. Jesus is God's One and only Son. To know Christ, you must believe that He is God in the flesh, just as it says in the Bible in John 1:1, "In the beginning before all time was the Word Christ, and the Word was with God, and the Word was God Himself." Yes, this may seem to be too simplistic, but you see God is not a hard complicated "try and see if you can find me," kind of God. God is loving, merciful, faithful, and His heart is for us—not against us. He wants us to know Him. He sent His Son, so that we could see in Jesus God's character, compassion, and His great love for us. Jesus freely gave His life for us as He willing crawled on the cross and took the punishment for our sins. He walked this earth as a sinless man, with all the same temptations that we have, but He did not give in to them. Because of Jesus, if we accept what He did for us, we have the opportunity to be called children of God.

Put the Pen to the Paper

Day 2

Lord, you are magnificent and my eyes are always toward you. David said in Psalms, "Bless the Lord, oh my soul and all that is within me. Bless His Holy name!" Blessing the Lord is what we do when we are His. His function for us is to breed holiness in His sight. Oh, how I love the Lord and His precepts! He is my God that I lean and rely on day and night. He is my King that I love and desire to be with, but I do not always put the effort and time in seeking Him. Oh my God, how I need your instruction and your guidance! Being obedient children is the desire of our Heavenly Father's heart. He desires our obedience to His instruction, prompting, and to His Word. The Bible tells us to delight ourselves in the Lord and He will surely give us the desires of our hearts, yes He will!

All I Am Is in You

Day 3

You have everything in this life according to My will. Your blessings come from Me. I am your provider, your coach, your guide, and your all in all. Promises from My Word are yours, take them and speak them for they are yours. As my Son, Jesus Christ, instructed His disciples when he told them that His will was to do the Father's will, so I instruct you. He did not do anything on His own. You shall live just as the Word says because apart from Me you can do nothing.

Everything that Christ did was from His Father's instruction and His leading. Jesus lived His earthly life in this way. He did not move until His Father told Him to move.

That is how I want My children to live, vitally connected to Me, walking with Me, talking with Me, and not moving without Me. For I the Lord have Spoken.

Prayer of Honor

Day 4

Father, great God of the universe, I give You all glory, honor and blessings because they all belong to You. For you, oh God, are great and worthy to be praised and worshipped. For You alone, God, are my God and there is none like You. None that can ever compare or stand in Your presence. For You are God, I Praise You and bless You, my God! Oh, King of Glory, have your way in me, have Your way. Lead me by your Spirit, by Your holy Hand. My God, my Savior, for I am Yours forevermore!

    Praise be to you, Lord! Praise, praise, praise, the Glorious King!

The Earthly Things

Day 5

The earthly things of this world are death and carnal. We are not to set our minds on these things because they will bring us down to death. Earthly things produce the fruit of unrighteousness. The desires of the flesh, which are sinful and lustful, will lead us to the path of decay and death. On the other hand, we should think on things that are above, the things that are pure and right in the sight of God. These are the things that will bring life and will flow out from you to others. Abundant life, that only comes from our Savior Jesus Christ. Jesus said that He has come to give us life and life more abundantly, but that Satan has come to kill, steal, and destroy. Ask yourself what things you should think about, life or death?

Lord, I ask that your Holy Spirit will give us discernment when our minds are going the wrong way. Please help us to turn to Your way of thinking.

By Faith

Day 6

Yes, it is by faith I live and breathe. Yes, it is by faith we speak out God's word and call it as so, even when nothing around us has changed. Yes, again it is by faith that we keep on praying, knowing that it is the only way of defense in this world. I praise God for that faith which He has imparted to us through His Precious Son, Jesus Christ. For if we had not believed on Him, this faith would not be in existence. So it is with a great big thank you, Lord, for this faith You have provided to us through Jesus Christ. Again thank you Lord!

The prayer of thanksgiving is another way, while we are in this world, to keep us from looking at our circumstances that are not changing. You know, another thing that does not change, is Jesus. It says in Hebrews 13:8 that He is the same today as He was yesterday and will always be. Praise the living God! Thank you Jesus, for we may receive by faith all You have done for us that continues forevermore!

Jesus Is My All

Day 7

When I say, "Jesus is my ALL," I really mean He is what ALL should be in my life. Now we know with the things we deal with day in and day out, that we allow Him to get lost in the routine of our busy lives and start focusing on the "me" things and the "I" things. Lord, I am not exactly sure how You do it, but I am thankful that Your Word says that Your grace is sufficient, and that our salvation does not depend on how many good works we do, how much time we pray, read your word or even seek your face. Because You know, Lord, my "want to" does not always line up with what I actually do!

My "want to" says, "Jesus, you are my All-and I need You despite the struggle to actually sit in Your presence and be still enough to hear Your voice. Thank you Lord for loving me anyway!"

Dressed With no Place to Go

Day 8

God's Word says in Matthew 5:9 that "Blessed are the peacemakers for they shall be called the sons of God!" Yes, the peacemakers, not the peacekeepers, for the peacekeeper pleases man and not God. The peacekeeper fears what man can do. The peacemaker fears what can God do and wants to be a pleaser of God and not man. God wants us to stand up to man and not cower. He wants us to be in the God given place of authority in Jesus Christ, and to move in that authority. God's Word says that He "has not given us a spirit of fear, but of love, power and a sound mind." Apart from God, we can do nothing, and I mean nothing. He has imparted gifts to us and apart from Him we cannot move in them. Fear of man separates us from what God has intended for us to be and do in His kingdom as part of His body.

As for being dressed with no place to go, wow, we have the full armor of God and we are to wear this armor as the children of God. However, if the enemy has taken our authority, because of the fear of man (intimidation) then he has taken our rightful place from us!!! He has also stolen what God has given us to impart to the body of Christ.

Jesus Lives

Day 9

Yes, Jesus is alive! The most amazing thing to me is that He lives in me! I know this is true because much of the "old me" does not exist anymore. The Word says "old things have passed away and behold all things have become new!" In my life, there are still some things that I am waiting to happen and praying to become new. God's Word says it, so I know it will happen. When Jesus lives in you, your "want to's" are not quite the same anymore. Yes, we still have to put down the flesh. It is natural for us to be sinful, and as such, we want everything in sight. Our natural man fights against what the Spirit of God wants, and if you have asked Jesus to come in to your heart and be your Lord and Savior then He does live inside of you.

You know if you ask Him, He really does come to make His home in your heart! He really wants to be your Lord, but we have to choose the path of righteousness. He will not make us go on that path. No, we have our own free will. It is our choice to ask Him to be our Lord and Savior and it is our choice, once we do that, to follow Him.

Following Him, is finding out through His Word how we are to act as a child of God. It is not saying a prayer of salvation and then doing nothing else. God's Word says if we want to please Him we must have faith. Faith does come. It comes through hearing the Word of God. The more you hear it, the more your faith will rise. Faith comes even stronger as you speak God's Word out of your mouth, and by hearing your own voice speak God's Word. Wow, that is wonderful!

The enemy of God is also our enemy because we are the children of God. The enemy does not want God's children to hear the Word, much less speak the Word, for he knows as we hear and speak God's Word that faith will arise in us. With the knowledge of God's Word, the enemy knows that his plans and devices to kill, steal, and destroy the children of God will be exposed.

It is very important for us to learn God's Word and to hide it in our hearts, for the days are evil. God's Word is alive, active and teaches us how we are to live and also how to live in Christ. Jesus died on the cross and rose again! He did this so that we may live a blameless life. He took our sins and washed them away with His pure spotless blood—which has no sin!

Yes, It Is Mine

DAY 10

"Glory is Mine" says the Lord. "There is none that can share this Glory of Mine. I Am He that brings it and I Am He that keeps it. For if it is shared then it is not mine at all. For I shall not share this Glory of Mine," declares the Lord.

"So in order for this to happen on the earth, all of My children that love Me and want to honor Me will always give all of the Glory to Me, their Father. For they know how much they can do without Me, which is not much. But when they are in Me, and I Am in them, and they move and breathe according to My will, they are excited about giving their Father the Glory—and all of it! For My children know that apart from Me they can do nothing. And apart from Me there is no glory of God showing up in their lives! Yes, the Glory is mine in all the earth," says the Lord!

My Father Is the Lord!

Day 11

My Father is the Lord of the universe. He is the One who is in control of everything. Everything on the earth is in submission to Him. But yet, He gives us, His children, the right and free will to choose WHO we will serve. He does not force us to do anything that our free will does not want to do. He loves us in spite of what we choose. Of course, He wants the best for us, and the best is to follow His ways, His Truth, and His plan for our lives.

Jesus came only to do the will of the Father. He said that His mother, sister, and brother are the ones who do the same. Yet, we have a choice, just as Jesus did. He chose to do what God sent Him to do, yet without sin. And because of His obedience, we are able to do above and beyond what we think—He did it all! He sacrificed His life, for our sins while making a way to the Father, which was broken by Adam. Now we can call the Lord, our Father, because of Jesus, the cross, and His pure blood which He shed for us! Yes, He is our Father, but not for what we have done, but because of what Jesus' free will bought for us. Salvation!

Jesus Is Lord

Day 12

Wow, the revelation that Jesus is Lord! Can you even comprehend exactly what that means? You know, right now my mind is so small that it does not fully understand this concept. But when God drops it into your spirit that Jesus is Lord, He is not just saying some random thought. He is making a statement that transcends all thoughts, understandings and realizations!

He is omnipresent. He is the God of the universe. Have you ever broken up the word universe? "Uni" means one, while the meaning of "verse" is word! Think on that for a moment. Especially since in God's Word it says that Jesus, the only "one" way to the Father, and that Jesus, the "Word," became flesh and lived among us! I do not know about you, but I am astounded and beside myself in wonderful awe when I ponder this thought!

By the revelation of God only, we know that universe means "one word" which is found in the being of Jesus Christ. In God's Word, John 1:1, it also says, "in the beginning, before all time was the Word, Christ, and the Word was with God, and the Word was God Himself." Now when we hear someone say Jesus is Lord, what kind of thought will you have about Him?

Reigning King

Day 13

Our God is the Reigning King of the universe. Do you understand what this implies? He is Ruler, He is Conqueror, He is Majesty, and He IS! He was always and is now continuing forevermore.

Now what exactly can our God not handle? Can you tell me? I can tell you that there is nothing that He cannot handle, at least unless you are handling it.

Do you know what it means to handle something? Well in my mind, I say it means to take care of it and do what needs to be done with something. But one definition states to handle something is "to touch; to feel with the hand; to use or hold with the hand."

Do we now see the problem of us handling our own lives? Oh Boy! If we would pray every morning before we get out of bed, "Reigning King of my life please handle it. I commit this day into your hands and I choose to get my hands off, and trust You in everything that comes across my path today. Lord, you are the Reigning King. Thank you Lord, that I can rest in knowing that you are handling my life!" Glory to God!

Sweet Surrender

Day 14

Sweet surrender is not something we are always ready to do. In fact, we fight, kick, and scream a whole lot before we even think about surrender. Surrender is only sweet when it is God to whom we are surrendering. God wants our surrender. He wants to be the One to guide our lives, but only when we trust Him as our Lord can we surrender to Him. You know you can trust Him to save you from eternal damnation. But, why, oh why is it so hard to trust Him as our Lord?

The Lord is what we need to have a fruitful life in the kingdom of God. How can we walk around claiming our salvation when we are only using it to get ourselves into heaven? Why would we not shine the light of Jesus in our lives? Why would we ever want to neglect the One who saved us?

Sweet surrender is allowing Jesus to be our Lord and by willingly doing what His Word says. Surrendering to Him means we are willing to spend time with Him in prayer, and listen for His promptings to know what He has in store each day. Surrendering is following His plan for our lives instead of our own! Can I tell you this is a daily struggle for me? The enemy of our souls hates us because we belong to God. The last thing he wants us to do is sit with our God, pray to Him, listen to Him, and follow Him! That is why when we finally surrender to Jesus as our Lord it is so sweet and comforting!

The Battle

Day 15

The battle is not ours, you know, it does belong to the Lord. We are to just put on the whole armor of God and be ready to go. The enemy does look around to see who he can devour. But, if we do what the Word says about putting on the whole armor of God, he cannot defeat us because we are hidden in Christ. When I say we are hidden in Christ it does not mean we are hiding from the enemy, no! We are not cowards! For God did not give us a spirit of fear, but He did give us a Spirit of love, a Spirit of power and the Spirit of a sound mind!

No, when I say we are hidden in Christ, I mean that we are saved by all He has done for us including dying on the cross for our sins, for He had no sin. He became sin for us, and then was punished for it, and what we should do is accept what He has done. It is for all to personally receive Him as their Savior. The Bible says if you confess with your mouth that Jesus is Lord, accept Him into your heart, and believe what He did was for you personally, then you, my friend, will be saved! Now that is the gospel of Christ, which is also called the good news! Because it is good news!

Jesus came to the earth as a man. He was fully man and fully God. He was ridiculed, whipped, and hung on a cross until He gave up His Spirit and died. He then descended to hell where He took the keys from Satan and defeated death. He then rose from the grave in full resurrection power and ascended up into heaven where He now sits at the right hand of the Father while making intercession for us!

Do you believe this is true? If you do, confess it out of your mouth! Read Romans 10:9-13, John 3:16 which show about salvation; Romans 6:23 prove the wages of sin is death; Revelation 3:20 tells us that Jesus stands at the door of your heart; Revelation 1:18 tells us that Jesus has the keys; and back to the armor of God, Ephesians 6:10-18 tells us that we cannot put on the armor of God unless we are saved.

Your "Who" Is not Your "Do!"

Day 16

Do you know that who you are in Christ does not depend on you and what you do? No, by all means no. Who you are in Christ has already been determined by the Word of God.

Do you know that the cross, and the power of it, is who you are in Christ? What makes up the power of the cross and what is its purpose? As I am writing this, I am waiting on the Lord to reveal to me what it is He wants to tell us.

The power of the cross is the power that defeated the enemy. The cross now denies the enemy's power; the cross took the enemy's place in defeating his purpose on this earth. The cross and the preaching of it have the power to defeat the enemy in the lives of people who do not have a clue of what the cross means.

"The cross is My Glory," declares the Lord, "it is what I used to give dominion back to My children as they receive what My Son did on the cross. Please now, do you understand the power of the cross, My children? Receive this power as you believe that it was My Son I sent to the earth to die that brutal death. Together, We defeated the power of sin and death with the great power of the cross that caused redemption to come to the earth.

Understand I Am He, and yes, We are three, Father, Son, Holy Spirit and We love you with and everlasting love."

So now we can see that our "do" has nothing to do with "who" we are in Christ! Wow! I am amazed again how the Lord uses this pen in my hand! To God be the Glory and Honor and Praise!!!

The Well Is Deep

Day 17

There is a well that is deep, and when I say deep I mean way down there deep. The only way to get to this well is to know God. This well is the depth of where life is located. The depth of life is to know the Life Giver. His name is Jesus. Also known as Messiah, Life Giver, Ruler, El Shaddai, King of kings, Lord of lords, Peacemaker, Healer, Teacher, Great Physician, My God whom I lean and rely on every day. He is Lord, and He is Savior of the world if you will have Him. He is the Well of Life, if you drink of Him, you will know Him. To know Him is to love Him, the more you know Him the more you want to know Him. He is the Gift of God that keeps on giving. His strategy is for you to come to realize your need for Him. Once you realize this you can drink, drink, drink and never grow tired of drinking from this wonderful well of Life He has to offer.

He is such an Awesome God, to which none can compare. He is Life! Without Him, the life we have is crumbling and lifeless. It leads to the things this world has to offer, where there is no satisfaction. Only God can satisfy our every need and want.

Without Him we are groping for anything and everything. Our need for Him is so immense we do not even realize the size of our needs. Until we have tasted of the Lord, we do not know how good He is for us. You may ask, "How do we taste?" Ask of Him, require Him as a necessity of life. Do not go anywhere without Him. Call on Him and come to Him. Cry out to Him. Ask Him to come to you and live inside of you. Give your life over to Him and let Him be the Lord of your life. It is then you will find out the depth of the well of life.

Go to His Word after you have called to Him and ask Him to reveal Himself to you. You ask, "Where do I read?" Start in the Bible in the book of John and read about how much He loves you!

Jesus Is the Lover of My Soul

Day 18

Many may say that Jesus loves us, but what does that mean to someone who does not know Him or know what He has done for them? I think instead of saying, "Jesus loves you," those of us in the family of God should show and prove how Jesus loves. Jesus does live inside of us, if you are saved. His Word says that they will know you by your fruit, and the love we have for one another.

Is that love coming forth in our daily lives? Are we allowing God's love to flow through us to others—especially to the ones that are unloving to us? Or are we looking and acting just like unbelievers, those who are not saved and who do not have Jesus living in their hearts? Boy, we need to take a picture of ourselves, in other words examine, to see if we are in fact loving one another and God as we do ourselves.

Jesus said that we are to be salt and light in the world. Salt preserves and light shows the way to Jesus in a very dark world. Are we obedient to His Word? I can say that I am not always very salty, and I am not always very bright with the light of Jesus.

Lord, help us be what you have called us to be, so that we can truly show people that Jesus is the lover of our souls. He touches souls through His children, His word, and by His Holy Spirit that draws them to Himself.

Rest in Knowing

Day 19

The King of Glory is our Father. He owns everything in the earth and everyone, but it is our choice to follow in His ways or to reject them. Why would we be so foolish to reject what is best and choose what is bad for our lives? My goodness, I know we are not doing this purposely, but we are deceived into thinking we are fine when in fact, when we are going our own way, doing our own thing, rejecting God. God is not rebellious, but it is we who are rebelling against Him.

God only wants the best for us. To get the best we have to follow in the best ways, which are God's ways. He loves us so much, that He gives us the choice to love Him, but we have to choose because He will not make us do anything. To love Him is to follow Him, obey Him, and want to please Him more than we want to please ourselves and others.

Then and only then, can we rest in knowing that He is the God of the universe and we are His children because we are striving to follow and please Him. His rest is not like physical rest; it is peace that comes from relying on Him. Our rest is the result of knowing that His mercy and His promises are who He is, and that He is the source of our rest!

Inspiration Has to Come

Day 20

I cannot move unless I am inspired by God. I cannot pray unless I am prompted by God. Why do I think I can write, unless God tells me what to write?

God is teaching me so much about my dependence upon Him. I need Him so desperately for every aspect of my life. I really cannot function properly if I am not leaning on Him. I must acknowledge Him in everything and make sure I check with Him about everything I do. I need to not forget about Him and try to figure things out on my own. When I realize how much I need Him, it is then and only then I can rest, trusting Him in what He has directed me to do or not to do.

Most of the time, I will fret over something I had no business fretting over in the first place. When I finally talk to God about it, He tells me to let it go and leave it to Him. If He wants me to do something with it, He will prompt me! This leads me to be at peace, and not worry or fret! Glory to God! We need to be watchful, for we become fretful, worried, frustrated, or aggravated when we cannot figure how we are going to handle something. Guess what? We are to bring it to God and ask Him what to do and then be obedient to His voice, not to the loud and demanding voices that are telling you to fix it!

God is not demanding, but He is correcting, loving, gentle, firm, and truthful. God is reliable, faithful, peaceful, restful, and He is everything we need. He is our guard and He will not lead us astray, but He will keep us and not let us go. He is awesome! He is all knowing and everything we need. He is, meaning always present with us forever. He is my inspiration. I need Him always for everything, and even when I forget, My God is always there waiting! Praise the Living King!

My Grace Is Sufficient for You

Day 21

Jesus said, "My grace is sufficient for you." Why not believe it? But at times, we ramble on, trying to do everything in our own strength. We forget that it is because of His grace that we are even able to come to a saving knowledge of Jesus Christ.

Why not believe that we are forever in need of His grace? Grace is not something we earned or something in which we can boast. It is and was freely given. It was given at salvation and Jesus has not taken it away. But at times, we forget about God's grace. We are not to act like babies all of our lives and continue to sin while claiming God's grace. Yes His grace is there, for when we need it. But, we are to grow and mature as Christians, feeding and strengthening our spirit man with the Word of God. We need to hear, do, and confess the Word of God out of our mouths. You know, we cannot grow and mature without food and water in the natural. But, as we feed on the Word of God our spirit man strengthens just as we would be by putting the most nutrient food in our bodies.

If we do not take in our spirit food, our spirit man who we are when we become born again, is malnourished cannot walk in the Spirit, for it is weak. So, we want to walk in the flesh, according to how and what the flesh wants in this life. The flesh only wants its way, and it wants it now. For example, if you see something in the flesh that you want, you get it. If you smell something in the flesh that you want, you eat it, for in the flesh there is no self-control. Self-control is one of the fruits of the spirit, as is goodness, kindness, patience, love, joy, peace, faithfulness and gentleness.

Do you know the yucky fruits of the flesh? The bad fruits of the flesh include: immorality, impurity, indecency, idolatry, sorcery, enmity, strife, jealousy, anger, selfishness, divisions, party spirit, envy, drunkenness, and carousing. The Bible warns us that those who do such things will not inherit the kingdom of God. Please read Galatians chapter 5 especially verses and 16-26, and ask God what He wants to reveal to you, for you.

We know that the flesh and the spirit fight against each other. This is why it is so difficult to discipline ourselves to read and study the word. The Spirit in us needs to take authority over the flesh that it lives in and make a habit of praying, worshipping and reading and studying God's word. Reading God's Word over and over will help us wait for God to speak to us personally, and you know He will! For His grace is sufficient for us. Grace means *underserved favor*!!

Lord, I Am Renewed

Day 22

By the power of the Holy Spirit, I am renewed. I feel that by God's Spirit, I am made fresh and ultimately more His than ever! This renewing does not come without sacrifice, but our sacrifice is nothing compared to what Jesus Himself sacrificed for us on the cross of cavalry.

Our sacrifice is something as small as not sleeping as long as our flesh wants, or spending more time in the Word and in His presence than our flesh wants to do. Boy, how foolish does our sacrifice sound compared to Our Savior, who allowed Himself to be beaten and tortured before He willingly hung on the cross for our salvation? Now, when you hear that, our sacrifice does not sound like a sacrifice does it? What does it sound like to you? I will let you answer that question for yourself.

You know, when we willing to come to the Lord, He is just waiting excitedly because we are seeking His company. He is especially excited when our motive is just to come to spend time with Him, not just because we want something from Him. We know how it feels when our children come to us continually to ask for stuff, but they really do not want to be with us. Those moments are not very exciting, are they? But, when they just want to sit close by just because, how we treasure those moments!

By the way, when we do just come to the Father, our time with Him is precious to Him and it does renew us and refresh us. His word says in Psalms 42:1, "as the deer pants for the water, so does my soul long for You."

What Can I Do to Please God?

Day 23

Let us see what the Word says about this question. First and foremost, God's Word says it is impossible to please God without faith. But what kind of faith is it, the faith that when you go to sit down in a chair, that the chair will hold you? Or is it the kind of faith that says "my God can do anything we ask, when we are abiding in His word and His word lives and abides in us, as long as it is according to His will." His will, by the way, is already written in His Word. God is not separate from His Word, after all, the Word says that Jesus is the Word made flesh, and walked among us. I believe this is the kind of faith God wants so that He can be pleased with us.

You know, when we are not looking to God and His Word that we are not in the kind of faith that pleases God. We are just out there with no foundation to stand on in our lives. Oh how important it is to our Father that we are walking in His pleasing faith by trusting Him. We can rely on His Word because it is truth. If we continually grasp this with all that we are, we will always be in the "pleasing God" kind of faith!

The mirror of the Word checks us for flaws as it corrects, directs, keeps, and tells us we are His Beloved. Why do you think it is so important to discipline ourselves to continually be soaking in the Word of God? The Word cleanses, refreshes and builds our faith as we hear ourselves speak it out of our mouths because faith comes by hearing the word of God.

My Trust Is in the Lord

Day 24

Trusting in the Lord is not always easy. When you consider what else is out there, there is really no choice. We could trust in ourselves and believe we have it all under control. But, what do we do when a crisis comes into our lives? Do we run to the nearest bottle of wine or pills?

We may cope that way, but when we do, it is our way of finding a false peace. For as soon as it wears off, we are right back where we started. And the vicious cycle starts all over again and again. This is where addiction comes in to play, when what we really want is love and peace.

Only a relationship with Jesus can give us this love and peace for which we are all searching. His ways are so much better than our ways. You know, Jesus Himself did not do anything unless He had direction from His Father. Well, if Jesus did not move until He first got directions, what make us think we should move until we hear from Him?

Pride tells us we could move, but pride is not of God. Pride in ourselves and thinking we are all that makes us independent from God. Pride says, "I don't need God. I know what I am doing and how to do it." Pride is what got Satan kicked out of heaven.

He wanted God's position and he wanted to be worshipped. Well, that kind of sounds like us and our selfishness. We may think it is our way or the highway, but that is not God's way.

His ways are so much higher than our ways! First of all, He loves us just the way we are so we do not need to change because He already loves us. Of course, He does love us so much that He does not want us to stay in the pitiful, prideful, selfish state that most of us are in when we finally realize how much we need Him.

He wants us to come to Him as we are and acknowledge our need for Him. As we do, His mercy, love, and peace comes to us. As we yield to Him, allowing Him to take the lead, we can follow. Boy, what rest and comfort comes to us as we become more dependent on Him. Our lives become more peaceful as we rely on Him. Instead of looking to ourselves in every situation, we should look to Him for help, guidance and direction. Then you will learn what His peace is like, and that you will not want to move unless you have God's peace. Guess what, that my friend, is how you trust in the Lord! You know, as I finish this writing, I am amazed at how good God is! I really love and trust Him. My confidence is in Him, for apart from Him I can do NOTHING! What about you?

Rest in the Knowing

Day 25

Our rest comes in "the knowing" of God's character. Who He is, what He is, and how He loves with an everlasting love. His love never runs out, never gives up, and always pursues us. His peace is so real, so tangible, so intense, and is like a mighty rushing river, but ever so gentle.

Yes, His rest is real. You can really rest, not like a physical rest because it is better than that kind of rest. It's a rest that comforts, knowing and trusting that He is your God; and that He loves you no matter what happens. His rest remains when nothing else will. His rest removes every burden that weighs you down and wears you out. His rest is real.

Come and enter His rest. Come to Him by acknowledging Him as your God, and by trusting that He will come to you. God's Word tells us to "draw near to God and He will draw near to you." Resting in His presence is better than anything the world has to offer. He is God and nothing compares to Him.

I Am Worthy Because of Jesus

Day 26

Do you know how much you are worth? Do you know God, our Father, thinks you are worth more than anything we can imagine? Our worthiness does not come from anything we can do or speak. No, our worthiness comes from the love of the Father. It was that most wonderful gracious love that sent Jesus to the earth. The only reason God, the Father sent Jesus, His only Beloved Son, was for us all; for you and me, personally.

Our God is a personal God. He is not someone way out there. He is our God, that never leaves us not forsakes us. He sent Jesus to us to rescue us from sin and death and separation from our God, the Father. The only reason Jesus came was to die in our place because of our sins. It was not because of His sins, because He had none. He did not have to die for us but He willingly did because of His great love for us, the sinners.

Do you know He loved us and came for us before we even knew Him? He came and took our sin and death and in exchange, He now offers life and freedom. We do not have to continually live in sin anymore! We can ask for forgiveness and He is faithful to forgive. We can ask for help in areas we struggle with sin, and He is there to help us. We do not have to walk this life like we are alone, with no one to turn to because Jesus came to our rescue. Not only did he come, but when He was resurrected and went back up to the Father, He sent the Holy Spirit to us. He also said we are to ask for the Holy Spirit to baptize us and when He does, His power will come upon us. Power to witness to others about what Jesus has done in our lives, power to not give in to sin continually, and power to live a holy life.

He also will impart the help and guidance of the Holy Spirit, for He is our teacher, our counselor, our help, and our comforter. He is also our wisdom when we have none. When we ask the Holy Spirit to come upon us, the evidence He gives us is that we will have a new language. It is called speaking in tongues, also known as the heavenly language. This language will not be fruitful to your mind. It is your prayer language that comes from the Holy Spirit, and when you speak it you are praying the perfect will of the Father.

This is a wonderful gift that Jesus sent us, and all we have to do is ask for it. The Holy Spirit will pray through you when you do not have a clue what to pray for or how to in your understanding. Sometimes when you start to pray in the Holy Spirit (tongues), the Holy Spirit will instruct you how to pray in your understanding! God is so good!

Can we even get a glimpse of how worthy we are to our God? How many of us would send our son or daughter to take the place of someone who did not even know they existed? Our God is that great and so incredibly loving! I am in awe once again!

Rest in Knowing

Day 27

"Rest in knowing the peace that you continually search for only comes through Me," says the Lord. We search continually for the things that will satisfy us. We think that things will make everything okay, but the realization is that as we continue to gather more and more things, yet we still feel empty. When will we realize that it is only a relationship with Jesus that satisfies?

Going to Church and hearing sermons is good, but unless you take it further it is just religion. Religion is something you do because it is expected of you, with no real commitment to the One they are preaching and teaching about at the service.

But, if you take your relationship deeper with Him, come to Jesus by setting time aside for Him, not because you have to, or because it is expected of you, but because you want and need to be in His presence. Being in His presence is where you find fulfillment. This is where you can be who you really are in Him. Sitting and resting with your Creator while opening up His Word is where you will find Him and He will speak to you, personally. This is what we hunger for, to be with the One who made us and to have fellowship with Him. Trust Him for everything—even your very next breath, for it is from Him that it came, and it is from Him that it continues to come.

Knowing where our rest comes from is VICTORY.

The Wait Is Real

Day 28

In the word of God, He instructs us to "wait on the Lord." For a very long time I could not grasp the understanding of what that entailed. But now I have come to the realization that to wait on the Lord is to be still and not move and wait until you hear Him speak to you. Another way to wait is to sit in His presence and just rest there. Also, before you act on any decision that needs to be made, wait on His promptings.

It seems we hear people say all of the time, "I'm waiting on the Lord," but what exactly are they waiting for? Waiting involves us! We are the ones who need to move to prepare to follow His leading. If we are not in the active role of actually waiting on the Lord, meaning spending our precious time with Him, and listening for His voice and instruction, then nothing will happen. I do not believe anything will happen, unless we actually wait for Him, for the waiting is real- and that is a reality.

When You Can Do Nothing

Day 29

When you can do nothing without Him, you're in a good place. You're in a good place because you are waiting on Him before you can move. The Word does say, "apart from Me you can do nothing." But it also says "abide in Me and I will abide in you." It also says, "I can do all things through Christ who strengthens me."

Yes, the waiting and the abiding. The abiding is living in Christ, and He in you, never to be apart. Think on that for a moment. The waiting, go back to the previous lesson for that one. The abiding is God's way of saying, "You are My place where I want to live and breathe and have My way of coming and going on the earth, working through your hands through your feet, and through your love for one another. Be My vessels and show the earth My way of living and being, for My Glory," says the Lord. "Yes, My way is not man's way but Mine," says the Lord.

Today Is a New Day

Day 30

Realism is today. Where you live is today. We are not to live in yesterday, tomorrow, last year, or even ten years ago. We are to live in today. Today is the day of salvation. It says in the Bible that today is the day that the Lord has made and we are to rejoice and be glad in it!

When we look at previous days or worry about the days ahead or years to come, the enemy has taken from us what God has given, which is today. Glory to God! God has given us a new gift everyday called today. He wants us to rejoice and live for Him today! He wants us to live in His fullest for us and for His glory. We are not to live worried, depressed, or gloomy, with no light of Jesus shining forth in our lives.

He says this is the day the Lord has made! Let us rejoice and be glad! This is something He is telling us to do today! So where is our rejoicing and gladness? It is not in our circumstances and it does not depend on our wants.

There is a choice to make today. The choice is to choose life or death. The choice is to live for God, which is eternal, or to live for our flesh, which is death.

My Life Is Not My Own

Day 31

My life is not my own, I've been bought with a price. What is that price you make ask? I will tell you it was and is the pure spotless, blameless, blood of my Lord Jesus that paid the price. He willingly gave His life for mine. All He wants in exchange is for us to accept His gift of love. He wants us to exchange our old, empty, unsatisfied, selfish way of living. His way of living is satisfying, because He made us and knows our needs more than we do. Check out His word. It is all laid out for us to receive, but we do not go after it; most of the time we are still trying to live our way. Jesus did not die for us to stay in our old sinful ways. He did not do all He did for us for us not to take advantage of all He paid for!

He paid the price for freedom from sin, bondage and living without Him. Come on! Let's take advantage of all that He has done for us! When we receive salvation, it is not anything we can brag about that we have done for ourselves. We had nothing to do with the price that was paid. It is a gift! When someone gives you a gift, you do not ask for the gift, they come to you and say, "I want to give you this gift."

Their gift comes from their heart; from their willingness to give. It comes from them wanting to bless you! You had nothing to do with them giving it to you. It was their choice to give, and do you know what? The only part you have in it is receiving the gift and being thankful for it. The rest is in your hands. Though what will you do with this gift? Will you use it to its fullest advantage or will you lay it down in a corner, wishing you could do something with it?

Jesus does not want His gift of salvation to lie in a corner. He wants us to take full advantage of His gift and to walk in the freedom He has paid for us. His gift was very expensive. We cannot even understand how He could have exchanged His perfect life for our sins. He paid the price before we even knew we would receive the gift of salvation. So, what are we going to with this wonderful gift of salvation? Will we share it with others, or do we keep it to ourselves?

You know and others need to know if we have indeed received salvation for our life is not our own!

Rest in Knowing

Day 32

Being pleased with me is not my best subject. I am usually aggravated with myself, because I did not get up early enough to spend, what I feel is adequate time, with the Lord. I hear Him telling me to come, but I go back to bed thinking I could use that forty-five minutes of sleep, so I just stay in bed. Then when I decide to get up, I beat myself up saying, "I could of, should of, but I didn't!" Unfortunately, this did not happen just once, but many times!

Our Father is gracious, loving, forgiving, faithful, and continues to call us. He does not give up. He does not get discouraged. He just loves, and loves and loves. He is ever ready to pour out His love upon us when we finally decide to become disciplined enough to come to Him when He calls. Sometimes we think we come to him when He's not calling!

However, you know that is not true, because His word says, we cannot come to the Father unless He draws us! All I can say is, "Lord, thank you! Thank you for drawing me to Yourself! Thank you, for loving me, and bringing me to your side! I love you Lord Jesus!

Rest in knowing!

My Dependence Is on the Lord

Day 33

I can do nothing on my own. I need to rely on the Lord, depend on the Lord, and lean on the Lord. He is my strength, for without Him I am weak. He who comforts me is my God. I love to hide myself in Him and rest. I can only do this when I come to Him, and He is always there.

He is dependable. The one sure thing in this life is our Lord. He does not change and He is faithful. He is my all and I cherish Him. He is my rest, for without Him I am restless. He is my comfort and my peace. Because of all that He is, if I believe, I will be overtaken by Him!

I Have Nothing Until I OBEY

Day 34

Rest in knowing that each time you obey the Lord your obedience is strengthened. There is strength in obedience. The weak do not obey. Obedience comes from determination to do what you were called to do.

Obedience is an act of our will. Actually obedience goes against what we want. Many times, we want our will to be done, not God's. But when we obey we are submitting ourselves under the authority of God, because all authority we are under is placed there by God.

As we submit to the authorities God has placed over us, we are in fact submitting to them as unto the Lord. Strength and preparation to obey God directly, comes from submission. Our submission to the Lord makes us strong. It takes strength to follow and obey Him, and He supplies that strength and willingness to obey. Jesus set the best example of obedience to the will of the Father, and we should strive to be like Him!

Nothing

Day 35

Nothing can take the place of spending time with the Lord. Nothing can compare to His presence. No one or nothing can compete with Him and win. Being in His presence is all we really need—it is a necessity of life. Just like we need food, water, and air, we need to be in the presence of the Lord. Being in the presence of God is where we are fed spiritually and where we are strengthened.

Without His presence there is no fullness, there is no comfort, no peace, no assurance, and no rest. So, why we do this to ourselves? This is self-inflicted. We do not have to be without the presence of the Lord, we choose to be without Him.

We choose to be out of God's presence by not putting the Creator of the universe into our daily lives. We do not give Him the first part of our day—unless we are in a trial and we think we really need Him. But the truth is we always really need Him! In reality, any problem that surfaces in our lives would look small if we were in constant communion with the Lord.

We need to come to Him daily to fill all of our needs every time one arises. Our priority should be to continually come to Him with our problems instead of trying to fix things on our own. He is the author and finisher of our faith. He knows the beginning from the end. What makes us think we've "got this" when we do not have a clue? The reason is because of the demonic names, pride and control, that want us to bow down to them. They want to be our gods. Yes, gods as in worshipping false gods.

Now, what do we do once they have been exposed and we understand more about our situation? First we are to submit ourselves to God, then resist the devil and he will flee from us. We can resist, all day long, and get very frustrated and weary. But when we learn to get under the covering of God by being obedient and submitting ourselves to God, the blessings start to flow and the enemy has no hold on us. It is when we are disobedient and want our way due to our own pride and wanting to be in control that the enemy has his way with us. Oh my! Do you see the difference?

A prayer we should say each day should be, "Lord, I choose to submit myself to you today. Please help me to be obedient in all your ways and aware of your leading. Help me Holy Spirit to walk in your direction and in your peace. Show me, Lord, where and when to resist the devil. Please Father, give me discernment to know the difference in the enemies schemes and when attacks will strike. I choose to stand firm in you Lord Jesus. In your Name I pray.

Today Is a New Day

Day 36

Today is a new day, glory to God! Yesterday is gone, and the old things of yesterday and yesteryear are passed away. All things are becoming new. Today is new in a way that we do not have to live the way we lived in the past. We are to live for God, from glory to glory meaning we are forever moving forward in Him, His ways, and His likeness. God brings us from glory to glory. He enables us to change into His likeness. The more we come to Him, the more we become like Him.

Young people sometimes think that their friends are so cool, and want to be like them. If they give into the temptation, at times they begin to hang around them more and more. They will begin to dress like them, smoke like them, drink like them, and speak bad things like them.

However, the same thing happens when someone hangs out with God! Spending time with an Awesome God leads to a wonderful transformation. No one or nothing can compare to Him! When we hang out with God, we want to dress to honor Him, be like Him, please Him, yearn for more of Him, and most importantly we want to love like Him. And we definitely want to speak like Him! We will say what He speaks, life and not death.

We will also want to heal like Him and worship like Him. We want what He wants. Jesus prayed, "not my will be done, but yours." We definitely want to pray like Him!

When we are with Him, we want to wait on Him and listen to His voice while enjoying His peace! We also want to be compassionate like Him! We want wisdom like Him because we do not want to be foolish anymore. We will desire his input on everything-not to be wise in our own eyes. We will want to turn entirely away from evil!

That is why our time with the Lord is crucial, and vital to our walk with Him. We cannot live in this world without the world taking us over, unless we spend valuable time with our Lord. We need to learn to be still, pray, (talk to Him), read His word and ask Him to show us what He wants to reveal to us. He is so precious and much more valuable than anything this life has!

There is nothing and no one that can ever take His place in our lives. There is no substitute for the King of kings and Lord of lords! He is the Almighty and our ever- present help in time of need! He is God the Creator and He loves us, little old us! He wants to be Lord of our lives and He wants us to come to Him always with every little need—not just the big ones. He loves us and He just wants us to love Him back enough to spend time with Him!

Waiting Is Important

Day 37

It is not difficult to spend time in the Word and time in prayer. But many of us find it difficult to become still and wait for the Lord. We usually need to be quiet to hear His still small voice. Most of us do not take the extra time to hear our Lord speak to us; whether it is through His word or through actually hearing Him speak to His beloved. Oh, how we cheat ourselves out of the most precious part of our time with the Lord!

Are we that busy? If so, we need to slow down! Why are we in such a hurry? Hurry, hurry, hurry—the enemy wants us hurried because he knows the blessing we will miss when we do not wait on the Lord. While we are waiting on the Lord we are resting, gaining His peace, comfort, wisdom, and whatever else the Lord wants to impart to us. We will pass up His impartation if we refuse to wait on Him and we will not have a part of Him!

We often wonder why we are stressed and have no peace. We face, what feels like mountains of worry, anxiety, fear, doubt, unbelief, sickness, and grudges. As children of God, we need our time with the Lord, but mostly we need our time of waiting for Him. His presence is where we are changed, for in His presence mountains melt like wax! Selah! Pause and think about that!

Sit at My Feet and Learn from Me

Day 38

There is no other place I would rather be, than at the feet of Jesus. When you come reverently to His feet, you are free to bring to Him everything you have been carrying and leave there. In exchange you receive His love and you can trust that He will take care of it all.

At His feet there is rest. There is no fretting there and no time for worrying or thinking about what others will say or do. At His feet is just you and God. At His feet you may enjoy His peace and comfort by yielding to Him. You will find great comfort in knowing your God is with you.

Coming to Him changes everything—it changes the weight you've been carrying. The weight falls off of you and lands at His feet. When you leave your problems at the feet of Jesus, there is lightness where there once was heaviness. Your shoulders can relax instead of straining and stressing over the cares of life. It is freedom. You may bring it all to Him because He took all of your burdens and they were nailed to the cross. As He had said before He gave up His Spirit, 'It is finished'.

He has taken care of everything we would ever have to deal with and it was nailed to the cross. In exchange we have His victory that He won for us. He is our conquering King, He even conquered death and the grave for us! We may now walk in His victory. Because of His resurrection power we are more than conquerors through Christ Jesus our Lord.

So we need to come to Him and rest at His feet. Come to Him in humility and accept everything that He has done for us. Thank Him always and in all ways learn from Him. Go to His word and feed on His Truth, which renews our mind. As Jesus said, "Blessed are they that hunger and thirst for righteousness for they will be filled."(Matthew 5:6)

Frustration

Day 39

What is frustration? What causes frustration? How do we get rid of frustration? Webster says this: the act of frustrating; disappointment; defeat; as the frustration of one's attempt or design.

What causes us to be frustrated, to the point of disappointment and defeat? It looks pretty plain to me now, but when you're in the act of frustration, you cannot see anything, but the disappointment, it's HUGE, isn't it?

It's when we are walking by sight, instead of by faith. It's when we focus on something or someone to be what you want them to be and they are not. It is when our focus is on the things of this world, instead of the things of God. And we wonder why we are frustrated.

Let's see what the word of God says how we are to live. Heb.12:1-4 Therefore, wince we are surrounded by such a huge crowd of witnesses to the life of faith, let us strip off every weight that slows us down, especially the sin that so easily hinders our progress. And let us run with endurance the race that God has set before us. We do this by keeping our eyes on Jesus, on whom our faith depends from start to finish. He was willing to die a shameful death on the cross because of the joy He knew would be His afterward. Now He is seated in the place of highest honor beside God's throne in heaven. Think about all He endured when sinful people did such terrible things to Him, so that you do not become weary and give up. After all, you have not yet given your lives in your struggle against sin.

Meditate on these 4 scriptures awhile. The sin Jesus gave His life for was not His own, it was our sin. Ours sin caused Him to want to be on that cross. He defeated death for us, He did not have to, He wanted to for the joy that was before Him, we are His joy we are what He died for.

It is His victory, He bestowed it upon us, we just need to walk in it.

Now, why frustrated and how do we get rid of it? Answer, we just saw it in the word of God—keeping our eyes on Jesus, the start and finish of our faith; Speaking to Him, depending on Him, coming to Him and to His word for guidance always.

Destiny

Day 40

God's destiny or our destiny, which shall we choose. It's not real easy, but I choose God's. God's is exciting because you do not know everything, only what He shows you, as you walk closely with Him. I do not think we can really know God's destiny for our lives, not all of it at one time, unless we are willing to walk closely to Him, so that we can get His direction, His input on every area of our lives. How can we know God's destiny for our lives, if we are not in close fellowship with Him.

We have to be willing to be still with Him, wait on Him, learn to hear His voice, and then follow His leading. Otherwise I believe we will be choosing our own destiny, trying to make things happen in our own strength. This is a sure way to wear ourselves out, and stress out.

I don't know about you, but I want God, and everything He has for me. I want to make a difference in the kingdom of God. I don't want to waste my life doing my own thing.

Now with that said, do we really want God's destiny? What shall we be willing to do to get there? Are we willing to follow His leading or do we even take the time to follow? Jesus said, follow Me.

Lord help us to follow You, to take the steps you take, as you take them, one step at a time, Father, for Your glory in the earth. In Jesus' Name I ask.

Your Dependency Is on Me

Day 41

Why is it that we always look to our strength first, instead of the Lords? Why is it that we have to fall first, before calling on the Lord? Why is it that we allow rebellion in us, to keep us away from what we know is good and right?

I don't know, Lord God, why? Self, that is why? King Self does not want to be told what to do or how to do it. King Self wants what he wants when he or she wants it. It wants to be on the throne of our lives, instead of God, It wants to rule and reign, it does not want to bow down to the name of Jesus.

How do we rid ourselves of King Self? We feed and feed and feed our spirit man, by the word of God, by praying, by waiting on the Lord, long enough to hear His voice, by worshipping Him, by praying in the Holy Spirit when you need strength and guidance.

Your Obedience Is Overwhelming

Day 42

When we obey the Lord, I believe it overwhelms Him with joy and satisfaction. Just as when our children try to obey us, we have a sense of "look at my daughter, while everyone else is being disobedience, my child is doing her best to obey".

It is very pleasing to us, and I know we are pleasing to our Father, the same way.

You know we don't always want to obey, our flesh fights against it, but our spirit man wants what God wants. We love Him. We show our love to Him by obedience, even when we don't want to.

We do have to put our flesh under the obedience of our spirit man, but when our spirit is not fed spiritual food, like reading the word, hearing the word, praying, worshipping, fellowshipping with other believers, and anything else that builds up our spirit, such as praying in the spirit, if you have the ability, if not, ask God to fill you, so that you too can build yourself up as Jude verse 20 says, also check Acts chapter 2.

Obedience is always at work in the hearts of God's children, just as disobedience is at work in the hearts that do not belong to God. Just as we were before we accepted Christ in to our hearts. That is why it is very important to renew our minds with the word of God to be transformed into the likeness of God's Son, Jesus.

About the Author

Sheila Green is a wife, mother and the office manager of a family-owned restaurant she and her siblings inherited. She and her husband Kevin have been married for more than 33 years and have a 13-year-old daughter Rebekah, whom she home schools.

Contact Sheila at sheilalgreen@live.com
or visit her website at www.sheilagreenauthor.com..

www.ingramcontent.com/pod-product-compliance
Lightning Source LLC
Chambersburg PA
CBHW070800050426
42452CB00012B/2417